The Punch Book of DOGS

The Punch Book of
DOGS

Edited by William Hewison

Robson Books

FIRST PUBLISHED IN GREAT BRITAIN IN 1984 BY
ROBSON BOOKS LTD., BOLSOVER HOUSE, 5–6
CLIPSTONE STREET, LONDON W1P 7EB.
COPYRIGHT © 1984 PUNCH PUBLICATIONS
LIMITED

First impression October 1984
Second impression November 1984
Third impression October 1988

British Library Cataloguing in Publication Data
available.

ISBN 0086051 306 8

Printed and bound in Great Britain by
Redwood Burn Limited, Trowbridge, Wiltshire

"*Charming, attractive, intelligent and entertaining pet seeks adoption by lonely person of similar make-up. Inquire within.*"

"The usual? I serve six hundred drinks a day and I'm supposed to remember 'the usual'?"

"To be honest, with a scent like that I don't care if we never find him."

HEATH

"A horse! H-O-R-S-E, horse!!"

STANLEY by Murray Ball

Being the adventures of the Great Palaeolithic Hero

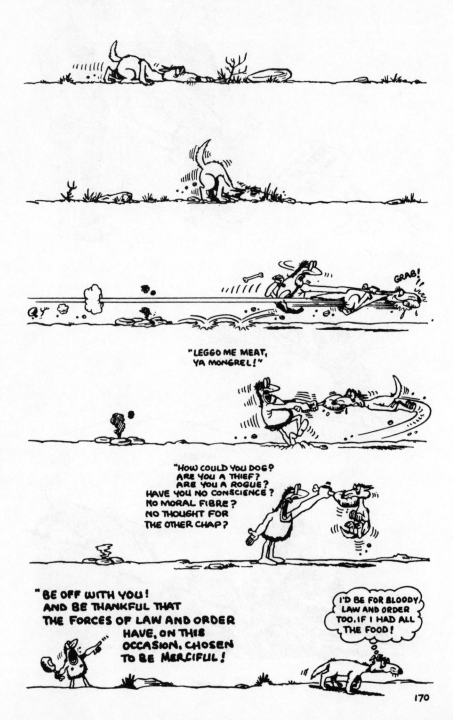

"Him? He's my bouncer."

"Here to discuss reincarnation in the studio, we have on my right the Reverend Norman Richards, and on my left, Attila the Hun."

*"Let's face it, his career's gone downhill since
he took up Pro-Celebrity Darts."*

"He'll have to be prepared to work nude, of course."

*"There was a vacancy for
your sort of act, but it
was filled five minutes ago."*

BANX

"Rex! What are you doing here? Didn't you get my memo?"

"I'm enrolled at the Kennel-Club—whatever a kennel is . . ."

"So, once he'd smuggled me through Customs, I thought, what the hell!"

*"She's absolutely marvellous. I am utterly dependent
on her for getting about!"*

"Well, I've been in three or four documentaries, two feature films and loads of commercials, of course. Mostly as a dog."

NSPCC

"Sorry, I'm a stranger here myself."

BANX

*"Don't lie to me, sir, you know perfectly well **which** guide dog."*

"Other men take their dogs for walkies."

"There are dogs in India that don't get that much to eat in a year."

"You see? He's a different dog when he smiles."

"Sit"

"Certainly not—you haven't yet worn out the one you've got."

"Of course, it's only a gerbil substitute, really."

"There are werewolves and werewolves."

"I must say, six months to see a leader is pushing it a bit."

"He followed me home—can we have him for dinner?"

"I think he's asking for asylum!"

*"How humiliating—personally I would rather
borrow or steal."*

"Here's the pedigree, madam; now may we see yours?"

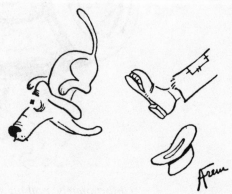

"I think I'm getting a chemistry set."

"Unfortunately, nothing succeeds like success."

"I suppose
that dog's over
eighteen?"

"We reckon it's probably the way he would have wanted it."

"Bogus calls to radio phone-in programmes help pass the time generally."

"He's not always so friendly with total strangers, but then he's not always drunk."

"If we're his best friend, how do the others get on?"

"Don't you think you're slightly overdoing your experiments on that poor dog?"

STANLEY by Murray Ball

Continuing the adventures of the Great Palaeolithic Hero

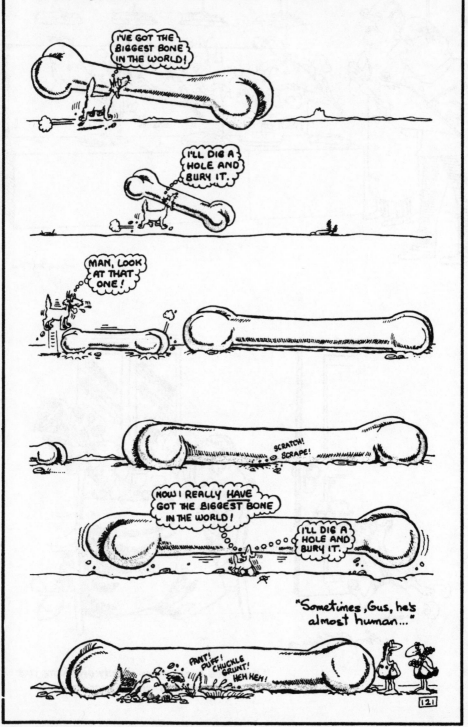

*"He was a **fine** dog."*

"And this is playful little 'Pepe' as he was when we found him wandering the Spanish back streets."

Goodbye Christmas, Hello House Training

GRAHAM charts the progress of man's best present

"Apparently tummy upsets aren't uncommon in young puppies."

"You know your astrakhan hat?"

"Now he's starting on the other or

"I just couldn't stand that pathetic whimpering from downstairs."

"*It's all right for you—off to the peace and quiet of the office!*"

"Just a precaution—somebody might step on him."

"Poor little thing—he's shaking all over."

" Still no luck with the advertisement ?"

"I didn't think the dog would take it so well."

"She won't eat, either."

"*My God! Instant reincarnation!*"

"Anyway, it makes a change from cats up trees."

STANLEY by Murray Ball

Continuing the adventures of the Great Palaeolithic Hero

"It is scientifically worked out. Supplying ideal amounts of proteins, carbohydrates, fats, minerals, vitamins; and promotes well-being and metal alertness. Now won't you try it?"

"He's far too self-critical."

"They've always got on wonderfully together."

"You just spoil that dog . . ."

"It took time but we finally got him house-trained."

"Why not admit it—you really wanted a budgie."

"I think he's gone off John McCormack."

"He's lost all interest in serious music since we bought that damn thing."

"Of course, that's always going to be one of the problems with stereo."

"The Provisional HMV have claimed responsibility."

"Well, I must say it's not my idea of an Irish terrier."
"P'r'aps not, Ma'am, but you must remember 'ow things 'as changed over there since they 'ad this 'ere Free State."

"Back, Watson—forward Mrs Woodhouse!"

"I must say, Mr. Baskerville, we had expected something larger."

*"My God, maybe it's a **genuine** Landseer!"*

"Did you hear something?"

"There, I was right—we have got a burglar."

"I'll show him who's boss—I'm going to switch off the electric blanket."

"He eats more meat than we do, but then,
we're not partial to postmen."

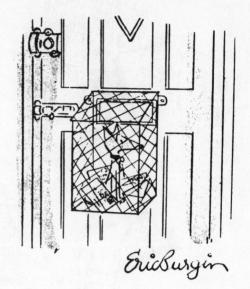

EricBurgin

"He makes a lot of noise but he's quite harmless really."

"All clear your side?"

"*In any case, we're not allowed to stop **on** a clearway.*"

"Ah, this must be the house."

DONEGAN

"For Heaven's sake, Edith, you're not going to send a card to the damned dog?"

"Margaret thinks it makes him look dependable."

*"As your best friend I shouldn't tell you,
but I'm going to. Your breath stinks…"*

"Actually Bernard likes to walk. It's the dog that needs a pint."

"You know the rules—no helping the dogs."

"It all started back in Kitzbuehel."

"You're lucky—I don't normally come out when I'm off-duty."

"Campari and soda, vodka and lemon, martini, lager, light ale. It's always the same when a coach party gets trapped up there."

"This is the dog that bit the cat that killed the rat that ate the malt that came from the grain that Jack sprayed."

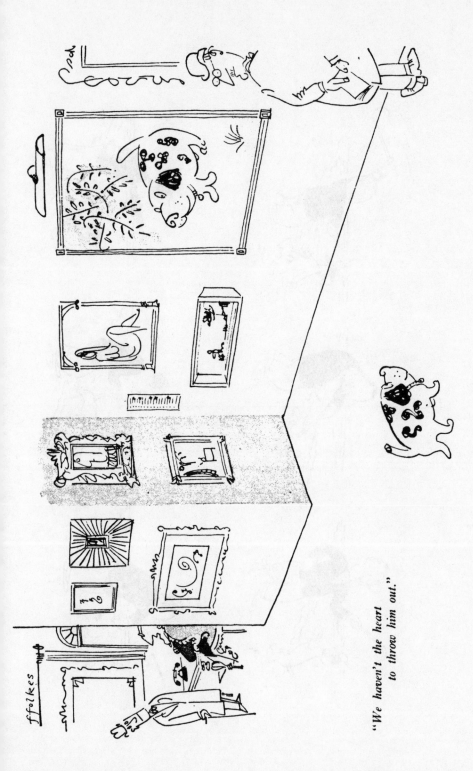

"We haven't the heart to throw him out."

THE DOG THAT DIDN'T

"I'm beginning to wonder if McDermot and his dog were quite as close as we were led to believe."

"This shape will do. Have you got it in a better quality fur?"

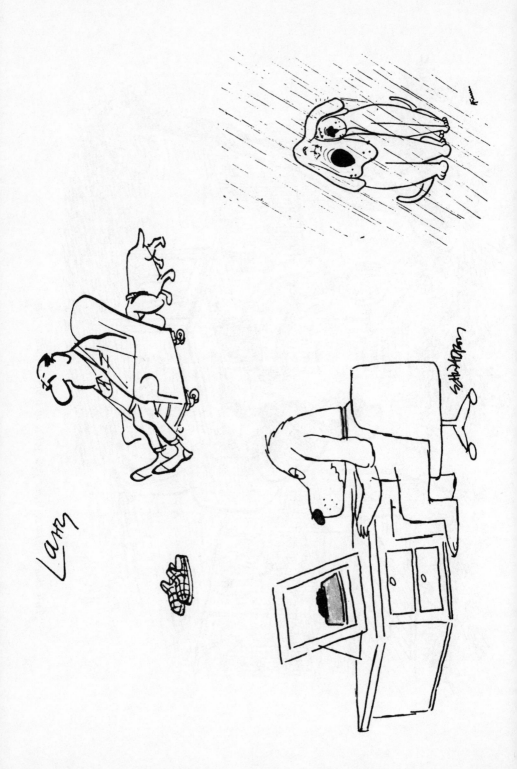

"You've been rubbing him the wrong way all evening."

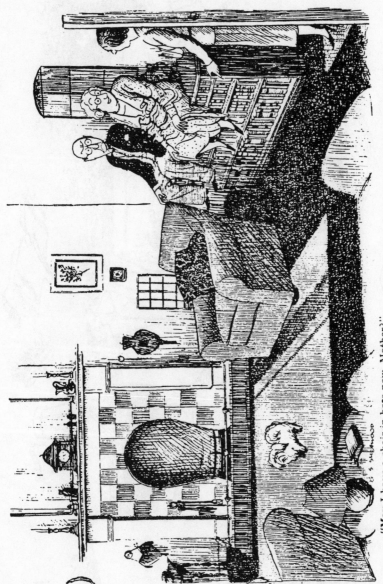

"May I have a chair in here now, Mother?"
"Just a little more patience, darling. Boo-Boo hasn't *quite* decided where he would like to sit."

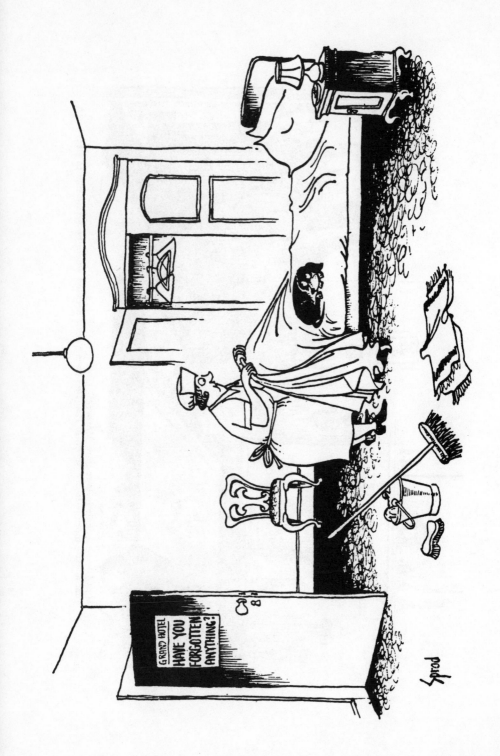

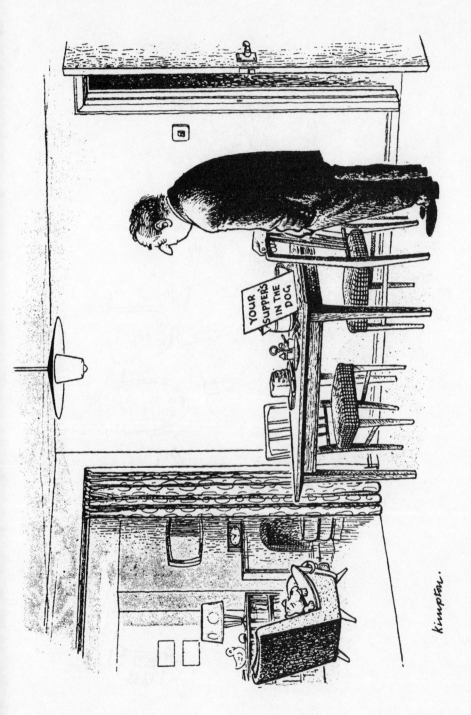

"It looks as if they didn't have the heart to eat the huskies after all."

"Who the hell do you **think** they belong to—who else but those blasted demonstrators!"

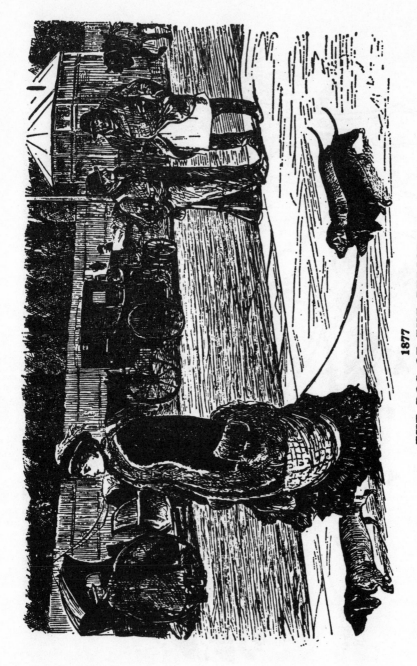

1877

THE DOG OF THE PERIOD

'I say, Bill! 'Blowed if she ain't a-been a-buying of her Dawgs by the Yard!'

"IT'S A LONG LANE THAT HAS NO TURNING!"

Small Boy (to timid Younger Brother). "COME ON, BILL! 'ERE'S THE END OF 'IM AT LAST!"

"Lionel claims to be the only white hunter living in Surbiton."

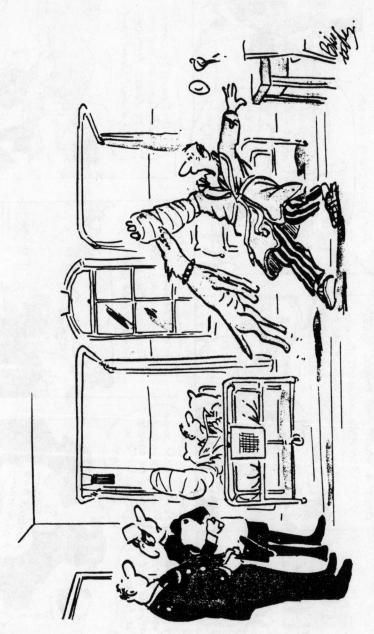

"By gum, Sister, that animal loves police dog handler Furnival!"

HANDELSMAN FREAKY FABLES

THE THREE DOGS

AN OLD SHEPHERD ONCE DIED (WELL, ONCE IS ENOUGH, REALLY), LEAVING ONLY A HOUSE AND THREE SHEEP TO HIS SON AND DAUGHTER.

Swop you my half house for your one and a half sheep?

Done.

Good day, sir! I happen to be mad for mutton and wool—swop you my three magic dogs for your three sheep.

What is so magical about them?

Don't take my word! Let them tell you.

They call me Salt: You want something to eat, Old Salt will get it for you.

Pepper is the name: You need somebody ripped to shreds, just whistle up old Pepper.

Mustard here: I chew iron.

Just to be sure I did the right thing—Salt, I'm a bit hungry—and there he goes...

WHOOSH

...and here he comes, with tuna salad on white toast, lettuce and mayo! Good boy!

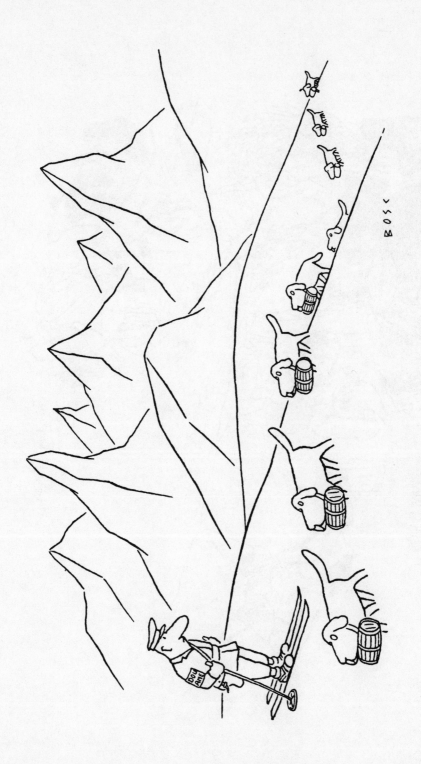

"Great news, Your Highness! The Kennel Club's thinking of naming a
spaniel after you!"

"I understand they're sacred."

"Shutting him in the kitchen was your bright idea!"

"Go and see what's bothering him. He doesn't usually howl for nothing."

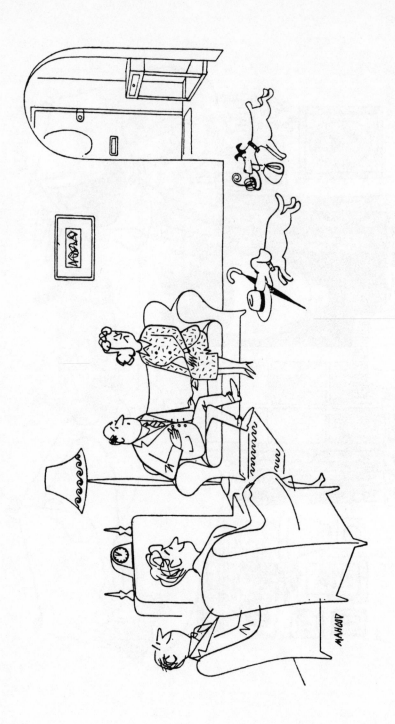

FREAKY FABLES by HANDELSMAN

smilby.

*"I wish you'd keep him under proper control, Mrs. White—
he's here again with his hypochondria."*

"I must say he's unusually small—even for a chihuahua."

STANLEY by Murray Ball

Continuing the adventures of the Great Palaeolithic Hero

"Nonsense! I'm sure it wasn't him!"

*"He **hates** having his claws clipped . . ."*

"Yes?"

"Like to see him do his 'Die for your Country'?"

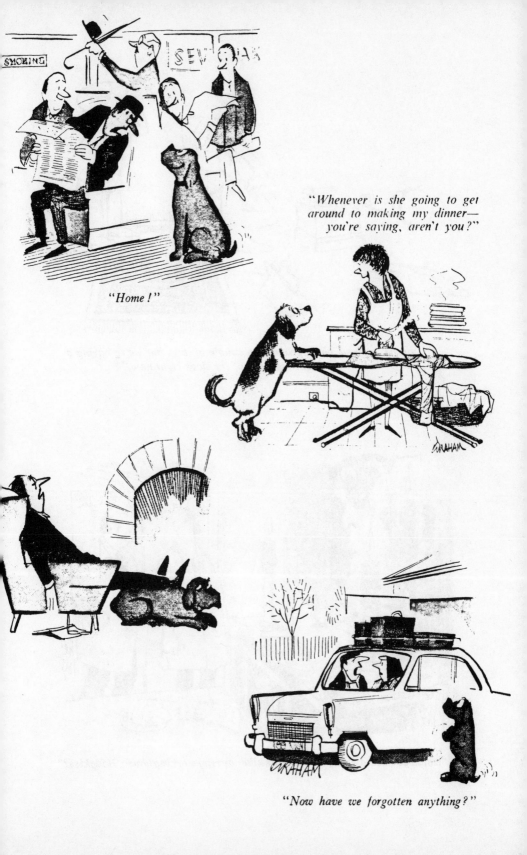

"Home!"

"Whenever is she going to get around to making my dinner—you're saying, aren't you?"

"Now have we forgotten anything?"

"I can fix up your phonograph in a couple of days but we're having a hell of a job getting hold of the dogs right now."

"Would you mind using the humane killer during working hours, Hodgkiss?"

"*Human life don't come into it, mate. We inculcate into 'em a healthy respect for property.*"

"*I feel he's over-confident.*"

"My God, man, that was the regimental chihuahua!"

"We compromised—my husband always wanted a dog."

"He's naturally a trifle upset at your having deserted him for two weeks."

*"Well, of **course** I'm surprised—I'm usually ignored at parties."*

"Well, dialect jokes, mainly—corgis,
alsatians, beagles . . ."

"Just remembering where he's buried his bones isn't going to be **much** of
a crowd-puller, is it?"

*"Remember, this is an important interview—**I'll** do the talking."*

"I couldn't face the club circuit so I took the desk job."

"It's worth a try!"

"Personally, I wish we'd stuck to rescuing rabbits from cosmetic labs."

"His wobbly head's jammed."

"It has reached our ears . . ."

MAHOOD

"*Registered.*"

*"Somehow I shall only feel we're really
in Europe when rabies has arrived."*

"Not the Johnsons' chickens again?"

"... Sit ... SIT ..."

"She bought it on the theory that owners grow to resemble their dogs."

"Go home, boy!"

"*Keeping a friendship in constant repair cuts both ways, you know.*"

"Hello, Guinness Book of Records?"

"He pipped me on presentation."

"Yes?"

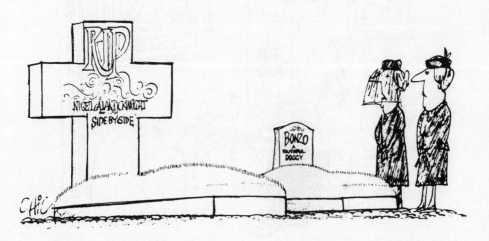

"They were devoted to each other, so I had him put down when Bonzo died!"

"*How would you like to come down to the office some day next week and see what makes a senior vice-president and treasurer tick?*"

That's very kind, Norris—but is it Art?"

"*Sit! sit boy! . . . sit . . . sit . . . sit!*"

"*Why, here comes Bill Firbright in three minutes.*"

44. Kennel Maid

Miss Beddington-Bulwer-Stride is a big name in doggy circles. A couple of years ago her young bitch Albertine Crozier ffanfair II walked, or rather hobbled, off with that supreme award of the dog-breeding world: Universal Champion of Champions. Miss Stride will never forget the excitement of that final judgement day as the betting odds veered and tacked between Doberman, cocker, beagle, pomeranian and peke—excitement among the spectators, that is, because Miss Stride herself was extremely confident that no other contender could prevent her zazouki from gaining that ultimate accolade. After all, it was her turn, wasn't it? Her turn for the citation and rosette, the doubled breeding fees and trebled puppy prices, and the loot from her endorsements of dog food, dog brushes, dog pills, dog deodorants, *et al*. Fido might be Man's Best Friend but he is also Very Big Business. Miss Stride's success with her zazouki is the familiar one. With her partner and companion (Miss Agnes Flint-Flint, a top name in poodles) she had run a very successful breeding kennel in the shadow of Box Hill where her efforts over the years resulted in the Miniature Great Dane, promptly accredited by the Kennel Club and now a firm favourite on Fifth Avenue and areas to the east of Park Lane. That success behind her, Miss Stride started looking for another piece of raw material upon which she could do a Henry Higgins. "Stroke of luck," she said recently. "Found the chap in Corsica. Aggie and I were on a mountain-walking holiday when I spotted her working the sheep. Terrific workers are Corsican zazoukis—run up and down the mountains all day, they will. Bright little beggars, too—the shepherd chappie just lets them get on with it. Naturally, I brought a couple home with me." At Box Hill the refining process began and now, ten generations later, instead of that little mountain dog Miss Stride has a lanky animal whose shape is "correct", but who also has poor respiration, hip dysplasia, weak pasterns, an overshot jaw, a docked tail and a highly neurotic disposition. "It's wonderful what careful breeding will do," she said, "My zazoukis will win prizes anywhere." But not in the Corsican mountains, of course.

COSTER (*reassuringly*). "It's orl right, mum. 'E's 'ad 'is breakfast."

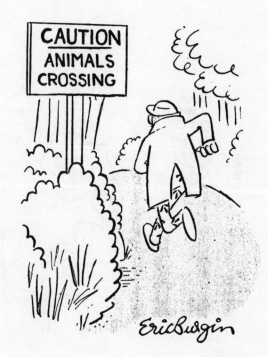

EricBudgin

"You'd think he'd test it himself!"

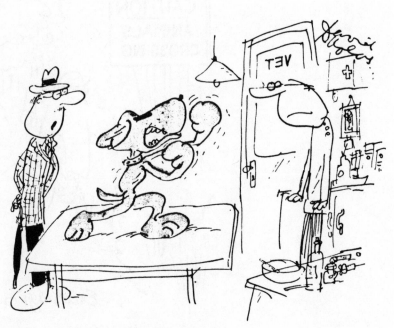

"He always seems to be spoiling for a fight."

*"I bet Barbara Woodhouse would be **really** proud of us."*

"As sniffer dogs go he's been a great disappointment."

"He's a good dog, but lazy."

"Two marks off for begging . . ."

STANLEY by Murray Ball

Continuing the adventures of the Great Palaeolithic Hero

"*I leave the whole of my fortune to my faithful dog . . .*"

"*The anti-dog lobby seems to be growing.*"

"... And I leave my faithful dog to my faithful secretary."

"Touching, be damned—it was a condition of the will."

POODLE

The name is a corruption of the original
German Pudel or Water Spaniel but this is a
description of its congenital urinary
dysfunction rather than any aquatic ability.
The dog was therefore exported to France
where it became a gundog for aristocratic
duck shooters who clipped the coat into the
modern pattern. This enabled the dog to be
used for wiping and polishing the hunter's
gum boots, the bare areas affording an
excellent grip. The Miniature Poodle was
bred during the Belle Epoque to service the
shiny boots of street-walkers. The Toy
Poodle is a typical answer to the perennial
Christmas present problem, but inserting the
key and overwinding can cause pain and
distress to all concerned.

PEKINGESE

The Chinese court favourite which was first
introduced to Britain in 1860 after the
sacking of the Summer Palace in Peking and
coincided with the opening of the first
Chinese restaurant in Gerrard Street.
Originally a long thin dog, the flattened face
and shortened body of the modern breed
were caused by the dogs being badly packed
on the long return voyage from China—
soldiers often jammed the animal head-down
into their kitbags and then piled extra boots,
books, bronzes and even cast-iron woks on
top of them. This may also account for the
Peke's bulging eyes and permanent bad
temper, but the irritating high pitched yap is
probably a reaction to being known as the
favourite pet of Barbara Cartland.

ST BERNARD

Renowned for rescuing lost drunks in the Swiss Alps, also known as the Good Samaritan for its habit of never passing a mugged ski instructor without giving him another good licking. Traditionally the dog carries a small barrel of VSOP cognac but recently, bowing to plebian tastes, younger dogs have been equipped with kegs of lager. However, the constant shaking in transit made opening the keg hazardous and many dogs and patients were blown away in the explosion. Alcoholism is an occupational hazard with this huge dog so beware of a drunken St Bernard, particularly in St Moritz where a pissed St Bernard still holds the speed record for the Cresta Run at 198 mph. It finally came to rest in Zurich.

IRISH WOLFHOUND

World's largest dog, sometimes standing four feet six high, though some Kerrymen have seen them as big as houses. Now only used as a mascot for the Irish Guards, the Wolfhound is a dog in search of a function, and attempts to convert larger specimens into racehorses failed when Paddy's Dream led the Irish Derby by twenty lengths, only to stop short and cock its leg against the winning-post. It was promptly disqualified for insulting the Archbishop of Dublin. A Wolfhound eats and drinks as much as five Wimpey labourers, but it does not sing maudlin songs about its mother. Strange as it may seem, the dog does not have a vote in British Parliamentry elections.

"In future, you'll wait until I tell you to shoot."

"Always makes that wheezing noise, does he?"

"Well, wherever he is, he's just dug up two dozen snowdrops!"

"You should have been firmer with him when he was a puppy!"

"I think he's trying to tell us something."

"This is Tarquin—he does impressions!"

"But I don't want a dog."

"You're ruining that dog."

*"She's a **wonderful** mother."*

thelwell

"McGinty must be near . . . that one's really fresh."

*"I'm afraid off the peg's
going to be difficult."*

STANLEY by Murray Ball

Continuing the adventures of the Great Palaeolithic Hero

"I'm just going to carry the dog around the block."

"Frankly, I feel he over-disciplines his animals."

"Here's my card. It has an area that you can scratch and sniff."

"He's got rabies."

*"It's his sad eyes and forlorn expression
they fall for."*

"Nothing personal.   It just hangs out."

"Here's the fifty thousand. Now hand over the cat."